# Forex:

## *Beginners Guide to Dominate Forex*

## *Table Of Contents*

are purely used for clarification purposes and no owners are in anyway affiliated with this work.

# Introduction

Congratulations on buying Forex: Beginners Guide to Dominate Forex and thank you for doing so. When it comes to maximizing potential profits, there are few better markets for doing so than Forex thanks to the power of leverage and what it can do to magnify otherwise minute movements. Where there is the potential for great reward, there is also the potential for great risk, however, which is why this guide was created.

The following chapters will discuss everything you need to understand the Forex market and how various events affect it in numerous ways as well as how to find the best online service to facilitate your trading needs. There is also a discussion of the importance of both technical and fundamental market analysis as well as strategies to utilize once the market has been analyzed. Finally, it ends with numerous extra tips to ensure that your Forex career starts off successful and only gets better from there.

There are plenty of books on this subject on the market, thanks again for choosing this one! Every effort was made to ensure it is full of as much useful information as possible, please enjoy!

# Chapter 1: Forex Trading Explained

Forex, often abbreviated as FX, is the shortened name given to what is known as the foreign exchange market or the currency market. It is the largest of all of the investment markets, currently doing more than 4 trillion dollars in trade per day. As a point of reference, the New York Stock Exchange only does an estimated 30 billion dollars per day in trade. Despite the size of the Forex market, the average individual trader was traditionally barred from participating due to the barriers presented by acquiring the right type of information from around the world at all times. The rise of online platforms for trading currency has changed all of that, however, and now it is easily available or anyone who is willing to take the time and the effort to use it properly.

## Forex is a speculative market

Unlike many other types of markets, when you complete a Forex market transaction you are not actually exchanging anything with the other party. Instead, the Forex market is purely speculative which means no exchange of currency ever truly takes place. Rather, the entire market exists as a number of computer entries that vary based on the price of the market in question. Each transaction that you make is then tracked and total profits and losses are then reported in your primary currency.

The Forex market came into being as a way for multinational mega corporations to easily convert currencies between regions without all of the red tape related to going to a traditional banking establishment. These corporations are constantly transferring money for reasons including things like payroll or vendor payments which means there is always something for speculative traders to speculate on. Currently only 20 percent of all Forex transactions are practical while the remaining 80 percent is all investors looking to make a few dollars in the process. Of this 80 percent, a majority comes from financial institutions and hedge funds with the rest coming from private individuals.

## Forex basics

When Forex traders make trades, they are actually trading a pair of currencies as opposed to stock or options trading where trading single assets is done regularly. This means that a Forex trade always involves selling one currency and buying another. Currency is traded in 3 different amounts which are referred to as lots. A micro lot is 1,000 of the currency you start with; for example, a $1,000 is a micro lot of dollars. A mini lot is 10,000 of the base currency and a standard lot is 100,000 of the base currency.

The smallest increment of Forex market movement possible is the pip which is a single percentage point or 1 percent of the total. It is often the most prudent choice for those who are just getting started in Forex trading to start by trading in micro lots because a pip of a micro lot is only a change of $0.10 to the price of the currency. This, in turn, ensures that early losses are going to be manageable when a trade ultimately does not go as planned. On the contrary, in a mini lot a single pip will equate to $1 and in a standard lot it is $10. It is important to keep this in mind as it is common for many currencies to vary by as much as 100 pips in a single session of trading.

Currency markets are driven by many of the same forces the traditional stock market is driven by and the biggest of these is supply and demand. When the world is in need of more a specific type of currency then the value of that currency will increase while if there is too much of a certain currency in the market then the price of that currency will decrease. Other important factors

7

to keep in mind are going to be things like, economic reports from world powers, geopolitical strife and various interest rates.

Unlike many markets that open and close each day, the Forex market is only closed on the weekend, starting Friday evening.

This doesn't mean that everything can be traded at all times, however, as the day is broken up into 3 different sections referred to as the United States, Asian and European trading sessions and while there is some overlap in regards to trading, the majority of the trading related to a specific region is doing during that region's time of the day. All currency trading is done in pairs which mean certain pairs are more profitable to trade during certain sessions. For example, those traders who tend to trade in pairs based around the dollar are most likely to make a profit during the United States session.

Another important factor that sets Forex trading apart from other types of trading is the fact that there are only 18 main currency pairs that are traded a majority of the time. This is not say that there are not any other pairs, just that the major 18 are comprised of only 8 currencies, (JPY)Japanese yen, the AUD Australian dollar, (NZD) New Zealand dollar, (CHF) Swiss franc, (GBP) British pound, (EUR) euro, (CAD) Canadian dollar and the (USD) US dollar. While this doesn't make Forex trading easier than other types of trading per se, it does make judging various options and managing your portfolio easier than in certain other trading scenarios.

## Other Forex differences

Aside from the differences outlined above, the Forex market differs from more traditional markets in other ways as well. One of the biggest differences is the fact that unlike many other markets, the currency market does not exist on a regulated exchange. This means it is not controlled by a centralized body of government and there are no guarantees on specific trades. There are no clearing houses to clear them and no way to have disputes arbitrated by official third parties. Instead, trades are based upon credit agreements, which can generally be considered the business equivalent of a handshake as it is less binding than a traditional contract but it works well enough as long as everyone plays by the rules.

This self-regulation tends to work quite well, despite its lack of traditional structure, because those who are trading in the Forex market must cooperate as much as they compete with one another if they ever hope to get anything accomplished. Additionally, in the United States at least, companies that deal exclusively is selling Forex trades deal with the National Futures Association which binds them to rules including those related to arbitration and fair conduct. For those in the United States, that makes dealing with a National Futures Association Forex dealer (discussed in detail in chapter 2) a no brainer.

Other differences include the fact that there is no limit on short selling as there is in the more structured stock market which means if you feel certain that a pair is going to go into a downward spiral then you can short it as much as you like. Also, there are no position size limits which mean that theoretically means you could sell a trillion dollars of currency at once if you had the resources and inclination to do so. There is also no such thing as insider trading in the Forex market, information, regardless of its source, is always fair game.

There are no traditional brokers, though the term is still used, in the world of Forex which also means there are no commissions because Forex is a principal only market. Firms who deal in Forex are dealers, not brokers. This means they are assuming risk related to the market and either buying from currency pair holders looking to selling or selling to those looking to buy. This means that instead of a commission they make money on the difference that the buyers are willing to buy for and the sellers are willing to sell for.

This setup also means that individual investors cannot attempt to either sell at the offer or buy on the bid when it comes to Forex. This is counterbalanced, by the fact that once you have made back the cost of your initial investment you don't have to

factor any additional commissions or fees into the equation as at that point, everything that you make is completely profit.

## Currency trading specifics

Currencies are always traded in pairs meaning that one of the pair is always going to be long, part of a positive market trend, and the other is going to be short, part of a negative market trend. As an example, if you sell off a standard lot of EUR/USD you would have then essentially traded euros for dollars which means you went short on euros and long on dollars. The most commonly traded pairs include EUR/USD (the euro and the US dollar), USD/JPY (the US dollar and the Japanese yen), GBP/USD (the British pound and the US dollar) and USD/CHF (the US dollar and the Swiss franc).

Additionally, there are 3 commodity pairs that are made up of countries that possess commodities in large amounts and, in turn, change as their commodities change. These are AUD/USD (the Australian and the US dollar), USD/CAD (the US and Canadian dollar and NZD/USD (The New Zealand and the US dollar). All told, these 7 pairs along with various other combinations including EUR/JPY (the euro and the Japanese yen), GBP/JPY (the British pound and the Japanese yen), EUR/GBP (the euro and the British pound) account for more than 90 percent of all the trades made in the Forex market.

## Currency quotes

When it comes to Forex trades, currencies are quoted in a very specific way. The first currency in a pair is typically thought of as the base currency while the second currency is considered the quote currency. Additionally, the US dollar is typically considered the base currency in that quotes are often written in units of $1 per the number of the other currency. These quotes will also always include a bid price as well as an ask price.

The bid is the price the Forex dealer will purchase the base currency for in the counter currency. The ask price is then the price the Forex dealer will sell the base currency for in exchange for a certain amount of counter currency. The difference between these two numbers is referred to as the spread. The major currency spreads discussed above are all written to the fourth decimal place.

## Additional lingo

Sterling, cable, pound: The 3 most common names associated with the currency of the United Kingdom.

Buck, Greenback: The most common nicknames related to the currency of the United States.

Swissie: The most common nickname for the currency of Switzerland

Aussie: The most common nickname for the currency of Australia

Kiwi: The most common nickname for the currency of Zealand

Little dollar, Lonnie: The most common nicknames for the currency of Canada

Figure: In Forex, any round number can be considered a figure.

Yard: This is the term given to a billion units of a given currency.

## More on margin

To be successful trade in the current market it is important to think about margin in a different way than you would if you were thinking about it in a more traditional sense. When it comes to the Forex market, the margin is no longer a down payment related to a future purchase of equity, it is instead a deposit that is made to your account that will cover future Forex related trade losses. In general, the higher the degree of leverage that a broker or deal allows, the greater the resulting margin is going to be.

When trading in the Forex market, it is important to always keep in mind that return is driven by yield. This means whenever you are purchasing one currency and selling another, the proceeds from the second transaction are affecting the first. You must also pay the interest rate related to any currencies you sell but gain interest on any currencies you buy.

## Rollover

In the Forex market, trades must be completely settled within just 2 business days. However, rollover is allowed in many instances which makes the process a little bit more fluid. A rollover is when open positions are pushed back 2 days in exchange for a certain percentage of interest for doing so. Rollovers can be used to give you more time to come up with a certain number of units but they are also traded on the Forex market on their own.

In any rollover transaction, the difference between the base interest rate and the counter currencies is visualized through what is known as an overnight loan. In this case, the trader would hold a long position in a certain currency that has a higher interest rate to gain the rollover. The amount gained from the rollover would vary depending on the day and the difference in relevant interest rates at the time. To avoid rollover, simply ensure that you don't hold any positions overnight.

## Leverage

In the Forex market, leverage can be thought of as borrowed money that is used to increase the returns of a specific investment. This money is borrowed from the dealer or broker that you will choose in the next chapter and rates of as much as 100:1 can be found around the world. This means that interested parties can control as much as 10,000 units of a specific currency by putting in just 100 units of the same currency. This can also backfire, however, as a bad investment at 100:1 can put you in a hole that will be difficult to dig out of successfully.

Leverage can be thought of as a magnification of the movement of the market. The losses that can come with leverage are often somewhat mitigated through the judicious use of stops as well as what is known as a margin watcher. A margin watcher is a type of software offered by many platforms that allows users to set parameters at which all of a certain holding will be sold to prevent catastrophic losses.

# Chapter 2: Choosing the Right Forex Broker or Dealer

As previously noted, the Forex market does 4 trillion a day in trade which means there are always going to be new dealers and brokers entering the competitive customer service space. This means that if you are ever hoping to trade in the Forex market, the first thing you are going to need to learn is how to judge the good ones from the bad; and what you want to consider when it comes to choosing the best one to suit your needs.

Unfortunately, this can be more difficult than it initially seems as different companies can phrase the same costs or benefits in different ways that can make the right choice especially confusing for new Forex traders. What's more, customer reviews can further muddy the waters as it's not always the truth, but the message of the most social media savvy that ultimately rise to the top. Luckily, there are a few things you can do to cut through all the heresy and effectively separate the wheat from the chaff.

## Broker versus dealer

It is important to understand that there are both Forex dealers, and Forex brokers which are used less regularly by smaller traders. Additionally, many Forex brokers are actually just Forex dealers using a term more people will recognize. When it comes to trading in the Forex market, you know you are working with a dealer, regardless of what they call themselves, if they are willing to trade with or against you in addition to setting up trades between their clients.

Brokers are actual middlemen who may even make trades for their clients while dealers are just professional trading firms looking to make money off of the spread. Brokers can be thought of as real estate agents, while dealers can be thought of as a variation of property wholesalers.

## Regulation

When it comes to finding the right broker or dealer for you, the first thing you are always going to want to look for is if they have the proper degree of regulation; including proof that they do so. Finding a regulated broker or dealer can be difficult depending on the part of the world you live in. It is worth it, however, as working with a broker or dealing without regulation opens you up to numerous additional issues that a new Forex trader won't want to deal with while still learning the basics of a good Forex trade.

The biggest of these without a doubt is fraud as unregulated dealers or brokers have no one to hold them accountable if they instead take your money, claim the trade went poorly, and go on their merry way. Even if the broker or dealer has the best intentions in mind, they are also subject to the same market swings that you are which means that if they go belly up, you will lose your deposit in the resulting mess as well. What's more, the laws protecting investors vary by area which is why it is important to look into the rules that apply to you directly before getting in to Forex trading. Failing to do so can leave you open to potential issues that you will not know about otherwise.

Regardless of the types of payment spreads that are being promised, the safer option is always going to be the best option.

## Capitalization

When it comes to deciding on the broker or dealer to help with your trades, the most important thing to consider after how regulated is the broker is the level of capital they have access to. With the increase in ready availability of online only brokers and dealers in the past decade, the number of these organizations that are a few unexpectedly subpar or outstanding trades away from financial insolvency has increased as well. This is why it is important to have a clear idea of just what your broker or dealer has access to as a way to ensure you are always going to get paid when money is owed to you.

To ensure that this does not become an issue for cautious traders, the Commodity Futures Trading Commission lists the current level of capitalization for all members and it is updated monthly at CFTC.gov. While many major markets are now requiring that brokers or dealers have a significant amount of capital in order to be in business, this is not the case with all online brokers and dealers so it is important to do your research if it is not clear where the broker or dealer you are looking at is based. If you are looking at an online broker or dealer you know is not based in the United States, then checking for any regulatory bodies in that country is likely the best way to start looking into their capitalization levels.

**Consider the platform**

As a new Forex trader, odds are, you likely don't have a Forex trading platform that you already have a preference for. There are countless trading platforms available at countless levels of quality that can make finding the ideal one for you a real pain, especially if you aren't quite sure what you are looking for. In this case, the best choice of action is going to be to seek out the MetaTrader 4 platform and familiarize yourself with it for now, until you have a clear idea of your own preferences to find something more specifically tailored to your needs. Luckily, most platforms on the market offer demo versions so you will be able to see them in action before you make any paid choices.

MetaTrader 4 is a great choice for new and experienced Forex traders which is why it is widely considered the most popular platform around to the tune of an 85 percent share of the market.

It offers a wide variety of features you won't be able to appreciate for quite some time, an easy way to important market indicators from the incredibly active user base and, best of all its free at MetaTrader.com. Head to the site, look through the features and see if it is a good fit for you. If it is, then you are going to want to ensure that whatever broker or dealer you end up using is compatible with it as well.

## Consider the cost

Regardless of what they are calling themselves, a good way to know if you are dealing with a broker or dealer is by the fee structure that they use. If their model involves a market maker, another term for the person who will sell if you buy or buy if you sell, then you know you are looking at a dealer who is going to make money based on the number of pips that separate the buyer's price and the seller's price. This will theoretically minimize your costs to just the level of spread that the deal offers, though some dealers have been known to manipulate markets to their advantage in the past. If your dealer is regulated you don't need to worry, however, as this sort of thing is closely monitored these days.

If, on the other hand, the Forex broker you are using is making use of the Electronic Communications Network to match your desired trades with the trades of others, then they will not take the other side of trades that do not have other customer takers. These types of trades will have a tighter spread as the broker is not taking a cut from this area and instead makes a traditional commission on each trade that is completed.

17

For example, if you find a pair that is AUD/USD that you feel certain is going to increase in value which means you are interested in pursuing a long position. If you are using a dealer, then you could likely buy the pair with a spread of 5 pips which means that AUD would need to move 6 pips in the right direction before you start seeing any real profit. If you are trading at a rate of $1 per each pip, then this trade would cost you $5. If you are trading standard lots, however, then this same transaction would cost you $50 so the lot size is extremely important to consider when it comes to finding the right brokerage or dealer.

On the other hand, if you are using a broker and the Electronic Communications Network for the same trade then you might come across a 1.5 pip spread as opposed to the 5 pip spread. Each trade would then cost, say $2.50 per trade which is a better deal for larger lot trades and worse for small trades as you still have to account for the spread as well as the commission costs which means what cost you $5 would now cost you $6.50; but the trade that previously cost $50 would now only cost $20 or $5 to open and close plus $1.50 for each of the lots.

In addition to the pure cost of each trade, you will also want to keep in mind the margin that each potential broker or dealer operates under. In the United States, brokers are currently only allowed to trade at a leverage of 50 to 1 (leverage is discussed in detail in chapter 3) which essentially means you have to put down anywhere between 2 and 5 percent of the cost down up front in order to place the trade. Worldwide, leverage can increase dramatically, up to 700 to 1 which is why it is important to know what margins your desired platform is operating under.

## Consider the available services

When it comes to finding the right type of broker or dealer it is important to have a clear idea of what they offer when it comes to the types of accounts available for users. Standard options include demo, micro, mini and standard and the primary difference is the size of the trade allowable from the account. This number will likely vary between various brokers and dealers, which is why it is best to shop around if you are interested in getting the best rate. Besides trade limits, the biggest difference between most accounts is the spread that will be charged by dealers and the commission rate that the broker will charge. Additionally, brokers typically throw in extra services for larger accounts as well.

It is important to not underestimate the value of a positive and easy to use customer service experience. When doing research, take note of how difficult it is to find a way to contact a real person, the harder it is, the lower the broker or dealer should rank in your mind. When you have a problem, especially as a new Forex trader, you are going to want to be able to get in touch with someone to help you solve it as quickly as possible, not after jumping through countless rings. Ensure you can contact your top choice in at least 2 different ways and for as many hours out of the day as possible. Remember, it is better to be safe than sorry, especially when there is money on the line.

Finally, many of the top online Forex dealers and brokers are starting to do everything they can to out-value their competition. This is great for you as it means that more and more additional services are being thrown in with even the most basic accounts, free of charge. As a new Forex trader this is especially useful for you since it means you can take advantage of education classes, improved signals, news and analysis all for simply showing up.

## Know what questions to ask

Once you have narrowed down your choice of potential brokers or dealers, there are a number of questions you are going to want to ask a real person representing the brokerage in question. Some of the questions you should already know the answers to, in these cases it is important to listen to how it is answered so you can get a better feel for the overall tone of the broker or dealer.

1. Which countries are you regulated in?

2. What currency pairs are available for trade?

3. Are customer deposits kept separate from operating capital?

4. Do you use the Electronic Communications Network?

5. What is your customer service like?

6. What trading platforms do you support?

7. What are the limitations of various account types?

8. What is the process like for withdrawing or depositing money?

# Chapter 3: Understand Analysis

Once you have an idea of the broker or dealer you are going to be using as well as the platform that you will be using for your trades, the next step is to understand how to analyze prospective Forex trades properly. This can be done in one of two ways, through the fundamental analysis or technical analysis. Fundamental analysis is certainly the more common of the two, though technical analysis has been enjoying a renaissance of late. It is important to always start off with fundamental analysis and then move to technical analysis.

At its heart, technical analysis is about starting off by looking at the charts while fundamental analysis starts by looking at relevant financial statements. Fundamental analysis believes that the numbers relevant to the market in question tell the whole story, while technical analysis focuses less on the numbers and more on the general market price. This inherently means that fundamental analysis takes longer than technical analysis though it is easier for new Forex traders to get started with. This time difference comes from not the time required to go over the information, but literally for the required information to get out to the public, which is often only a handful of times per year.

## Fundamental Analysis

Fundamental analysis is used to determine a broad idea of what the market will be doing in the near future based on numerous variables and changes in monetary policy from around the world. The end goal is to determine which currency pairs are going to be the most effective in the time frame that you are interested in specifically.

Establish a baseline: To start analyzing the fundamentals, the first thing you are going to want to do is establish a baseline to work off of. The baseline of your analysis should involve global macroeconomics if you hope for it to be effective. When setting up your baseline it is important to start at the macro levels so that you are able to collect all of the data that will accurately describe the pairs of currencies you are looking for at the micro level. Past behavior is a great indicator of future performance in this case which is why this process so effective.

When looking at past data it is also important to determine the various phases that all currencies go through time and again. The first of the phases is a period of booming success where volatility decreases and liquidity increases on a global scale. This is inevitably followed by a bust period where liquidity decreases and volatility increases. Understanding what phase a given currency is in is crucial to making the right choices at the right times.

Find the point in the cycle: To decide on the current phase of the cycle a specific currency is in, the first thing you are going to want to consider are default rates around the world. This includes reserve accumulation levels at international levels and the current rates associated with bank loans and other significant economic powers. These indicators will only appear once a phase is underway, but it is still useful to consider because the market reacts slowly to such things so you will still have time to use the information in question if you act on it quickly.

Consider global factors: Once you have a clear idea of what the current economic phase is for a given currency, the next thing you will want to consider is what, if anything, is currently going on that can create a relative economic expansion that will relate to the currency in question. This doesn't mean looking or obvious signs of economic turnaround, it means going above and beyond and looking at world events with an eye towards the future and what, if any, applications it might have towards economic growth in a specific region. This is especially relevant when a new technology catches on in a big way or when an existing technology moves into a new area that is primed for massive expansion in the near future.

These types of gains, when it comes to productivity, will typically generate a boom phase that will last until the technology has been fully absorbed by the new market which marks the end of the boom and the beginning of the bust. During the bust phase it is important to be as cautious in speculative markets as possible to prevent loss. Stick with smaller leverage points and decrease long term positions until currency pairs have bottomed out. Alternatively, if things are currently in a boom phase you are going to want to increase your risk portfolio and increase risk allocation to maximum amounts.

Consider the monetary environment worldwide: Outside of general worldwide patterns, the next thing you are going to want to consider is a variety of more specific factors including things like monetary policy in an effort to determine just how long the current boom or bust phase is going to last. The first thing you are going to want to consider is the current interest rates the major global powers are currently offering. This means when it comes to institutions including the Bank of Japan, the European Central Bank and the Federal Reserve, you are going to want to consider things like policy biases as well as their legal mandates. In doing so, you can get a clear idea of the supply growth of money they are experiencing which will throw other variables including interest rate expectations, market volatility and the growth potential of emerging markets into stark relief.

Compare the current rates with previous periods: Once you have a clear idea of what the current state of the specific fiscal policies in question are like, as well as what they were like in the past, you can then compare the two to get a better idea of how likely the current phase is going to continue for. Keep in mind that there is easy money to make when just coming out of a period of bust, as long as the traditional channels for credit are still available. If this is the case, then you are going to want to consider increasing your risk tolerance. On the other hand, you are going to want to decrease your level of risk of risk tolerance proportional to the distance you currently find yourself in relation to the height of the economic boom.

Determine volatility: When it comes to determining the level of volatility that can be expected in the Forex market for the relatively near future the best course of action is to look to the stock market. The Forex market tends to be more stable, the more stable the stock market is because the lower the perceived overall risk is, the lower the amount of perceived risk that can make its way to the Forex market. Volatility can vary greatly, even in a market with a well-defined phase so it is always best to hope for the best but plan for the worst.

Remember, the closer to the peak of the boom phase you currently find yourself, the lower interest rates, default rates and volatility will be, which means it is the best time to increase your level of risk. Alternately, the closer you find yourself to the bust phase, the higher the overall level of volatility, default and interest rates are going to be.

Decide on the best currency pairs: With a good idea of where the market currently is and how long it is likely to stay there, all you have left to do is determine the most effective currency pairs to actually sell. To do this you must first consider any gap between the two currencies when it comes to interest rates. You need to have a clear understanding of where each of the pair are currently and how likely they are going to remain close together and with a proper distribution between them.

To find this information you are going to want to start by looking at the difference in output gap as well as related unemployment statistics. When capacity constraints increase, while at the same time unemployment decreases, this shortage will lead to an inflated economy, which in turn, will cause interest rates to rise until the economy begins to cool. Charting this information will allow you to accurately determine the likely interest rate movement from the pair in question.

Additionally, you will want to consider the payment balance of the nations related to the currencies in question. The healthier the debt to capital ratio, the stronger the chances the related currency is likely to remain in times of crisis. To determine this amount, you are going to want to consider the capital as well as the current account and the general situation of each. This will help you to determine if the position the nation in question is having is due to asset sales or bank deposits or other, long term potential developments including things like accumulation of reserves or foreign investment.

Trade: When in a growth phase, the stronger the fundamentals of currency are, the more likely it is going to be sold compared to those that have higher interest rates as they are more likely to attract capital via interest rates that are higher. As such, the boom phase, specifically at its start, is the best time to sell currencies that have strong fundamentals and low interest rates while buying currencies with higher interest rates to balance out subpar fundamentals. At the same time, you are going to want to purchase currencies that have low interest rates and strong balance payments and sell those with high interest rates and weak payment balances if you are currently in the bust phase.


## Technical Analysis

When it comes to understanding technical analysis, the most important thing to always keep in mind is the action a certain price has taken in the past is likely going to be a reliable way to predict its action in the future. Because the Forex market goes for 24 hours a day, 5 days a week, this means there is always quite a bit of information that can be sifted through when it comes to finding the relevant information that can help you determine how a given currency pair is likely going to move in the future.

This makes it easy to use what are known as technical tools, things like indicators, charts and trends to achieve the reliable rate of success that successful Forex traders require. While the ways to do so can be quite complicated at times, at its heart, technical analysis studies supply and demand in an effort to decide what trend, if any, is likely going to continue moving forward. This is crucial for long term Forex success as the tools that technical analysis provides will increase the reliably of each of your trades nearly every single time.

## Core assumptions

The goal of technical analysis is not to simply measure the given intrinsic value of a particular currency, but rather to use the tools at your disposal to pick out beneficial patterns related to future activity that others may not yet have noticed. At its core, technical analysis functions by assuming three things to be true. First, the market will always discount anything; second, prices will always move according to trends; and finally, history will always repeat itself eventually.

The market will always discount anything: While detractors say that technical analysis is only concerned with the movement of currency price and little else. In reality; technical analysis assumes that the current price of a currency is a reflection of everything that is going on that could possibly affect the currency which makes it an accurate way to assess overall value. This then takes into account the broader economic climate as well as the current phase to determine when a valuable opportunity comes along.

Price will always move according to trends: If the current value or price of a given currency is said to move according to an established trend, this means once you can clearly determine a trend when it comes to past currency performance, you have a much greater chance of seeing that same trend repeat itself when compared to the chances of an entirely new trend; or the opposite trend occurring instead. Technical trading strategies tend to assume that this is always the case if they are going to work effectively.

History will repeat itself eventually: If prices move in trends, then it naturally stands to reason that technical analysis believes that as far as currency prices go, history will always repeat itself. This can be chalked up to the fact that those who participate in the market are likely to always respond the same way to similar market movement. This is plotted using chart patterns in an effort to determine these trends at their start when they can be capitalized on to the fullest. While some of these charts have been in use for over a century, they are still relevant when it comes to how the public reacts to price changes.

## Understanding trend

When it comes to using technical analysis effectively, it is important to understand trend and how it factors in to effective analysis. A trend is any general direction that you can see on a chart which indicates the direction the market is going to head in next. Some trends can be strong and obvious and others can be largely obscured because they are weak, as such, it is important to not discount patterns that might be hard to see at first, though you will need to be careful that you don't create patterns that aren't really there.

27

This is easier said than done, as price rarely moves in a single direction for a prolonged period of time and instead typically moves in clumps of lows or highs. As such, it is often more beneficial to track just these highs and lows and leave out the middle as a type of meaningless static. This doesn't mean that all your highs or lows need to be grouped together; instead, what you are looking for is a pattern of overall higher amounts compared to previous amounts. Likewise, for a negative trend you are going to want to look out for lows that are lower than previous lows and highs that also trend downward.

An uptrend is a positive trend and a reversal is a negative trend. There are also horizontal trends where the highs and lows balance each other out in such a way that there is no negative or positive growth.

Additionally, you are going to want to keep an eye on trend length which can either be short-term, intermediate or long-term. The longer the trend has previously lasted, the longer you can expect it to continue to last, as long as the other indicators remain the same. Shorter trends can actually be a part of longer trends, take a broader look and try and see the forest for the trees. To make this easier, it is important to take a look at the proper charts, for example, daily and weekly charts for a multi-year period if you hope to find long-term trends. On the other hand, daily charts are going to be a better choice when it comes to short or intermediate trends.

Once you have found an interesting trend, the next step is to draw a trend-line which is as simple as drawing a straight line that illustrates the direction the trend is heading. When it comes to an uptrend you want to draw the line so it connects the dots of the lows so the line is beneath the relevant data. If it is a reversal trend then you want to draw the line so it connects the high points, leaving the data underneath the trend-line. This line can be seen as the resistance level of the market which is the maximum amount it is likely to move the next time it moves. This line doesn't indicate how likely the next move is going to be a gain or a loss, just how much movement it will likely contain.

Channel lines are a pair of lines, one on either side of the data that indicate both general levels of resistance as well as support. One trend-line connects the highs, the other connects the lows. The resulting channel can move either up, down or sideways but the interpretation is going to remain constant. The goal is to establish a long enough channel to show a break from the data eventually, this break is likely the time to strike as there will likely be extreme movement at that point. It is important to always look for trends so that you can trade with them, never against them. The sooner you can identify a trend, the more you can make in the process.

## Analysis versus efficient market hypothesis

As a general rule, technical analysis is at odds with what is known as the efficient market hypothesis. According to this theory, the current market price is always going to be the right one as any relevant information in the past has already been absorbed into the current price. Because of this, theory states spending time using technical analysis to determine pairs that are currently undervalued is a waste of time.

The efficient market hypothesis can further be broken down into three parts. The first is weak form efficiency which states that all information related to the past price is already a part of the current price, so future movement cannot be predicted by past indicators. When it comes to semi-strong form efficiency, fundamental analysis is also called into question when it comes to finding future investment options. Finally, strong form efficiency says there is no way of analyzing the market because the market is always going to be at a unique point that will never be duplicated.

The arguments for and against the efficient market hypothesis are many and vast, certainly too vast to get into thoroughly here. It is simply important that you be aware of the divide and do your research before choosing the side that makes the most sense to you.

# Chapter 4: Forex Strategies for Beginners

Once you have a clear idea of what you are looking for and how to find it, you will be ready to start utilizing the strategies outlined below when it comes to actually making Forex trades.

## Carry trades

The carry trade is one of the most commonly executed strategies in the Forex market because it is as easy to execute as it is effective when used properly. Essentially, a carry trade is little more than purchasing a currency you expect to produce a large yield, and funding the purchase with a currency that offers a low yield. If you have ever bought low and sold high, then you know enough to make a carry trade.

Popular carry trades tend to involve currency pairs such as the New Zealand dollar and the Japanese yen or the Australian dollar and the Japanese yen, pairs that tend to have a very high spread when it comes to interest rates. This makes the first step of finding a high and low yield currency pair much easier. For example, if the Japanese yen currently had a .1 interest rate while Australia had a 4.5 interest rate then one would want to buy AUD/JPY on the currency market.

One of the reasons that the carry trade is so often effective is due to its ability to earn interest every day a long carry trade is being implemented with a triple payout occurring on Wednesdays to balance out the days of the weekend. To find the daily amount of interest you will be earning, you start by taking the interest rate of the long currency and subtract the interest rate of the short currency from it. You then take that number and multiply it by total amount you have invested in the current trade after leverage has been applied. Finally, you divide by 365 to find how much interest you are making each day. For example, take AUD/JPY and you invested $100,000 you would (.0450- 0.001) x100,000/365 which would result in about $12 per day in interest gained as long as interest rates remained the same.

## Using carry trades properly

This strategy caught on quickly worldwide because between the years of 2000 and 2007, the AUD/JPY pair routinely traded at an interest rate differing by more than 5 percent. While this wouldn't be much in most cases, in scenarios where leverage was routinely reaching 200:1, it was creating vast windfalls and losses at a staggering rate. This doesn't mean that they are still useful at all times, and knowing when it is actually appropriate to use a carry trade often separates the successful Forex traders from the failures.

Carry trades are at their best when major banks are either raising their interest rates or have announced plans to do so in the near future. This then typically results in lots of people jumping on the same carry trade, driving the disparity in price even further. The goal is to be aware of this trend as early as possible to ensure you get in early enough to see a big return on your initial investment. This is what is known as capital appreciation and being aware of when to use it effectively can have you seeing big returns in a short period of time.

Additionally, you are going to want to make a point of using carry trades when the overall market volatility is low as it is during this period that other traders are likely going to be the most comfortable taking risks. This is especially true of the major players in the market such as large hedge funds because as long as the underlying price doesn't decrease, everyone will continue to make money.

On the contrary, carry trades are not the right choice when it seems likely that the higher interest rate nation is going to cut their interest rates. This in turn makes foreign investors less likely to choose the currency pair to go long on which in turn means the pair will be less in demand, which then triggers a larger round of sales. The same goes for when the average annual yield is exceeded by the amount the exchange rate drops. Additionally, if a central bank directly intervenes to change the direction the currency is currently moving in this will make it a bad time to attempt new carry trades.

## Don't forget the basket

While the common carry trade can be useful if there are clear indicators in the currency pair as to how interest rates are going to be moving in the near future, if things aren't so clear then a basket carry trade may be the best solution. In this instance, it is important to instead purchase six currencies instead, the top three pairs, when it comes to interest rate disparity. This controls losses while at the same time ensuring a reasonable amount of profit, regardless of how many other variables turn out. While the amount of capital required is going to be greater, it may not be as great as it might first appear because you can generally get away with a smaller lot for all three pairs that still return a reasonable profit once leverage is taken into account.

The carry trade strategy is a good choice for beginners, especially those who might not have as much time to devote to trading at the moment as they might like. They will still be earning interest each day, and any changes might be a ways off, so if life gets in the way it is less of a life or death situation. As long as attention is paid to the general interest rate difference, sitting on a currency pair can actually be the right choice.

## Fibonacci Retracement

To use a Fibonacci retracement, the first thing you are going to want to look for is a market that is trending. The general idea here is to go long on a retracement, a temporary reversal of direction in the price of the currency, at a specific level when the market is positively trending and to go short on retracement when the market is trending in the other direction. To find a retracement level you are going to want to find moments when pricing indicators you are looking for reach high, or low, points that are higher, or lower, than the average high, or low point.

To understand the Fibonacci ratios that are useful in Forex, it is important to understand the basics behind the Fibonacci numbers which were discovered by the man whose name they bear; they start off as 0, 1, 2, 3, 5, 7, 13, 21, etc. Essentially, to find the next number in the sequence you simply add the previous 2 numbers in the sequence together. Now, if you measure the ratio of each number to the following number in the sequence you get the Fibonacci ratios that are used in forex. These start off as .236, .382, .5, .618 etc. While the exact reason that Fibonacci ratios apply to the Forex market isn't completely clear, it is clear that they resonate throughout the world at large from the smallest instance in individual molecules of DNA to the grandest in the organization of the planets in the sky.

Luckily, when it comes to utilizing the Fibonacci ratio in your trades, you don't need to memorize these numbers as all Forex trading platforms will have a tool that will do the calculations for you. This means that all you really need to do is to learn how, when and why to use them in technical analysis. It is important to keep in mind that Fibonacci levels are going to act as resistance as well as support for the price in question. As the price increases, the Fibonacci levels will act as resistance and as the price decreases they will act as support. Additionally, much like with regular support or resistance they can be broken.

To make use of the Fibonacci ratios on the charts you are going to want to start by finding the bottom as well as the top of the previous trend. If the previous trend is negative, then you will want to create Fibonacci levels starting at the top and moving downward as well as drawing the lines so that they will ultimately cover the next ongoing or completing trend. If it is instead a positive trend you will want to start at the bottom and work up. When creating Fibonacci lines, it is important to wait until the trend is fully matured as the process will not be accurate otherwise. If you feel as though you cannot accurately measure the completed time frame at the current scale, perhaps using a smaller scale would be more efficient.

Once you can see the lines in question, then you want to keep them in mind as time progress. If you choose a long position, then you will want to be especially aware of the moments the price reaches a point that is close to the Fibonacci level as this is when it is likely to start moving in the other direction, meaning it is time to cash in on your positive trades. The opposite is also true when it comes to short positions. If the prices break the Fibonacci levels then the price is likely going to decrease as a result, understanding the indicators that Fibonacci levels provide is key to using them effectively.

# Chapter 5: Tips for Success

## Understand the risk

When it comes to accurately assessing the risk of a given trade in such a way that you don't lose your starting capital, it is important to always have a clear estimate in mind as to just how likely it is that the trade in question is going to ultimately end in success. This means having a clear idea of what the technical analysis is as well as fundamental analysis, if possible. You will also want to determine the current mood of the market and have a clear idea of just what is going to happen if things start going your way, as well as what will occur if they don't.

After you have decided that the initial amount of risk seems worth it, it is then important to manage the potential for risk as thoroughly as possible. At this point it is important to try and increase the odds of your success by starting to determine an exit point that you will cut your losses at no matter what. The difference between the point you enter and the point you are committing to getting out at no matter what can be thought of as the total amount of possible risk for the trade in question. If that level of risk seems unacceptable to you, then you need to reconsider your parameters as there is no other way to decrease your overall level of risk.

Additionally, you are going to want to determine a firm exit point at which you will be happy with the overall return that has been generated, and get out regardless of how appealing riding the profit wave until it crests may be. Instead it is better to move to sell off half of the relevant currency, while setting a new and improved exit point for the remainder of the currency so you can split the difference when it comes to the risk as well as the reward.

When this happens you dramatically reduce your overall risk when it comes to sticking with the trade while it is on an upward trend.

When measuring risk, you are also going to want to be aware of liquidity to ensure there are always enough other sellers or buyers who are willing to work with your trade. As long as you are trading the major pairs, you will never need to worry about liquidity.

Finally, you will want to consider the individual risk of each trade that you make which is based on the amount of capital for trading specifically that you have available. Ideally, you want your risk per trade percentage to be as small as possible, and for new Forex traders you should start with trades that are around two percent of your total amount of trade capital. This means that if you have a starter bankroll of $5,000 then a losing trade would only set you back $100. Think of it this way, if you stick with the two percent rule, you have to make 50 bad choices in a row in order to completely run through your starter capital.

This also means that you are going to start out by trading mini lots wherein a single pip of movement is only worth $1. If you have a 50 pip margin for risk, then you are saying that you are comfortable losing $50 if the market does not move in the way that you predict. This means you can trade two different mini lots before hitting two percent of a $5,000 starter capital.


## Have the right mindset

When it comes to becoming an expert Forex trader, there are going to be numerous skills that you will need to practice in order to become successful. Nearly every other skill you will learn will fall to pieces, however, if you haven't learned how to keep your emotions in check while you are trading. A good trader often has to make split second decisions with little warning which means that you need to count on yourself to make the right decisions when it matters most. This, in turn, can only be done if you put your emotions away and let the facts guide you to success.

This is easier said than done, however, as a few bad trades are all it takes for many Forex traders to lose their ability to maintain perspective, especially when a particularly profitable trade takes a sudden and unexpected turn for the worst. This is always folly, however, as only by having a plan and sticking to it no matter what can you ensure that you are reliably profitable more often than not.

Likewise, it is important to do what you can to ensure that you never let fear enter into the equation, especially when you have a trade that has suddenly changed directions significantly. While watching your profits melt away can be scary, it is important to react first and let yourself feel regret over what happened later on, once it can no longer do anything to negatively affective your trade percentage. Fear can often lead to overreactions, which, in turn can lead to drastic overreactions in situations that would otherwise have more or less managed to blow over. When you feel the fear begin to well up, take a moment to determine where the root of the fear is coming from and it will be easier for you to react to it in the appropriate fashion.

Finally, it is important to never let yourself get sucked into the trap of overcommitting past your exit point in an effort to squeeze as much out of a specific trade as possible. This type of behavior is only going to lead to larger losses in the long run, as sticking around on the wrong trades will lead to a decrease in profits just as often, if not more as it will additional profits.

What's worse, the amount gained is never going to be worth the risk because the added profits are likely only going to be a small fraction of the overall hole before you exit anyway. While it will be difficult to walk away when there is essentially money on the table, it will get easier with time. Practice makes perfect.

## Be clear on the right approach for you

When you first start trading in Forex it is important to have a clear idea of what your general aversion to risk is as well as how you handle your emotions when it matters most. You then want to choose time frames and strategies that align with your natural inclinations rather than changing your personal comfort level to suit a plan that someone else claims worked for them.

To start, you are going to want to consider the time frame you are primarily working in and make sure that it aligns with your temperament. If you are looking for lower risk, then short time frames are a good choice. Otherwise, if you are instead looking to spend less time staring at a computer screen something longer is probably the right choice.

## Consider your methodology

After you are comfortable with the time frame you have chosen, you are going to want to find a type of methodology that works for you and stick with it. There are countless different methodologies from working with breakout prices to buying support, selling resistance, trading via indicators and more. The right methodology for you depends on your temperament as well as the timeframe that you are working with.

Once you find a few methodologies that you are interested in learning more about, the next thing you will want to do is to try it out in an effort to determine how successful it is going to be in your hands. You are going to want to stick with those that you can manage a reliable success rate of around 50 percent or higher. This means you are guaranteed to make money as long as you stick with the plan reliably and use it properly. It is important to test a wide variety of strategies once you get used to the basics as you never know when you will come across something new that works great with your own personal paradigm.

## Be realistic

When they are first starting out, one of the biggest things that sabotages new Forex traders is an unrealistic of the view that the future holds. This means that you need to be realistic in terms of what to expect when it comes to returns on your trades. The shorter the time frame that you are working in, the less likely you are to see major profit. By this same logic, trading in micro lots is always going to result in fewer profits than trading in standard lots. If you are currently unsatisfied with the return on your perceived investment you can either increase the amount of risk that you find acceptable or you need to have a larger amount of capital on which to draw from if you hope to increase your returns without increasing your risk.

Along these same lines, it is important to have a realistic idea of how likely it is that a given currency pair meets the qualifications of your chosen strategy. The right trades don't come along all the time which means there may even be days that you watch go by without jumping into the market. The more risk you are willing to take, the greater the number of acceptable trades you find, the more adverse the risk, the less you will be trading, it is as simple as that.

## Know who to follow

There is major money to be made in Forex and the bigger traders often make trades that can affect the market all on their own. Ideally, you always want to be in line with these players to ensure you are always with them and never against them. While it seems like it would make sense to follow the hedge funds as they are paid to make investments for others, the reality is that their style of investment doesn't often work for individual traders. As such, there are actually better options to choose from.

The first major players in the Forex market to keep in mind are the banks themselves. This is especially relevant in the spot Forex market as the Bid price is the price that those major institutions are willing to purchase certain currencies at. While sometimes these banks stand to make more from a losing trade for a variety of reasons, in general if you are on their side when a particular trade goes down it is likely that it will end in your favor.

You will also want to be aware of what major governments are up to in the Forex market as they tend to use it in much the way that the major companies it was created for do. The amounts that these entities tend to move is often enough to cause a significant change in the market's response. While you won't always want to trade the same direction as specific countries, you will always want to be aware of these trades and how it is going to affect your trades as well.

# Conclusion

Thank for making it through to the end of Forex: Beginners Guide to Dominate Forex, let's hope it was informative and able to provide you with all of the tools you need to achieve your goals now and for the months and years ahead. Remember, just because you've finished this book doesn't mean there is nothing left to learn on the topic. Becoming an expert at something is a marathon, not a sprint; slow and steady wins the race.

The next step is to stop reading already and to start deciding which dealer or broker to use, how you are going to apply technical versus fundamental analysis, and what strategies you are going to use the most. Once you find a few specifics that work for you, it can be easy to stick with them no matter what, especially if they were difficult for you to find initially. Don't be afraid to experiment, however, you never know when a new and improved system could be just around the corner.